Gabriela's Dance Recital

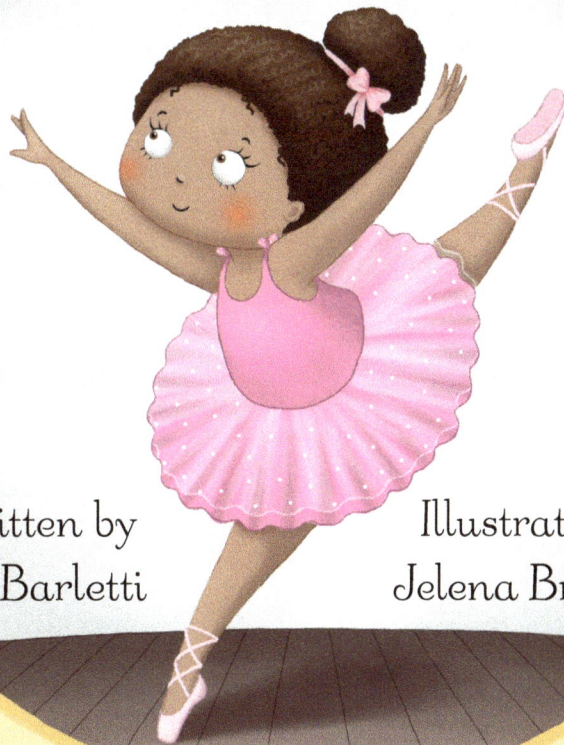

Written by
Jill Barletti

Illustrated by
Jelena Brezovec

El recital de danza de Gabriela

Gabriela's Dance Recital was adapted from the award-winning, bilingual personalized children's book *Dance Recital*. This adaptation was customized to reflect the author's bilingual family. We hope you enjoy it!

Snowflake Stories' award-winning, bilingual and single-language personalized children's books are available in any one or two of the following languages: English, Spanish, French, Portuguese, and Italian.

For more information about this book or any of our other offerings, please visit **www.SnowflakeStories.com**.

ISBN: 978-0-9909960-4-0

Published by

Snowflake Stories, LLC
115 Pocono Road, P.O. Box 125
Brookfield, Connecticut 06804
USA

www.SnowflakeStories.com

Printed and bound in the United States of America.

Gabriela's Dance Recital

was adapted from the
award-winning, bilingual
personalized children's book

Dance Recital

Create & order your
custom storybook today at
www.SnowflakeStories.com

Gabriela Montoya was a pretty, young girl.
Whenever she heard music, she would dance and twirl.
Little Gabriela loved to dance so very much.

Gabriela Montoya era una niña muy bonita.
Hacía piruetas cuando escuchaba musiquita.
A esta niña la danza tanto le gustaba,

She took dance class, practiced hard, and such.

que tomaba clases de danza y mucho practicaba.

But Gabriela's dance recital was drawing near.
And little by little she began to fear,
"What if I forget my steps or if I fall?
What if no one likes my dance at all?"

Pero el recital de danza de Gabriela se acercaba.
Y poco a poco de dudas se llenaba,
«¿Y si me caigo u olvido de algún paso dar?
Temo que mi danza a nadie le vaya a gustar».

Suddenly the doorbell rang. She thought for a minute,
"I wonder who's come to the house for a visit."
The sound of the doorbell helped clear Gabriela's head
of all of the feelings of fear and dread.

De repente el timbre de la puerta sonó.
«¿Quién habrá llegado?», Gabriela pensó.
El sonido del timbre la ayudó a olvidar
pensamientos de miedo y la mente aclarar.

On the stairs Gabriela listened. She didn't say a word
because downstairs, familiar voices she heard.
Had her grandparents arrived? It had to be!
Gabriela raced down the stairs in order to see.

No dijo nada y en las escaleras se quedó,
porque abajo voces conocidas Gabriela escuchó.
¿Habían llegado sus abuelos? ¡Eso tenía que ser!
Gabriela bajó las escaleras rápido para ver.

"Cutie pie!" said her grandma, all aglow.
Grandpa asked, "Are you ready for the show?"
Gabriela replied, "I'm very nervous, I fear."
But Nana said, "You'll be fabulous, my dear."

«¡Corazón!», con una sonrisa su abuela exclamó.
«¿Lista para el recital?», Grandpa preguntó.
Gabriela contestó, «Temo estar bastante ansiosa».
Pero Nana dijo que Gabriela estará fabulosa.

Her grandma continued, "You are only five years old.
You have to be confident; you have to be bold."
" 'I can do this,' you just have to think,"
Gabriela's grandpa said as he gave her a wink.

«Sólo cinco años tienes», continuó su abuela sonriente.
«Pues, ten confianza y sé valiente».
«Sí que puedo", es lo que tienes que pensar»,
su abuelo el ojo le guiñó al comentar.

To the living room they went to sit down for a chat.
They talked about this, and they talked about that.
When the time came and goodbyes were all said,
Gabriela's grandparents gave her a kiss on the head.

Ellos fueron a la sala para conversar.
De todo un poco pudieron hablar.
Cuando sus abuelos se despidieron,
un beso en la cabeza a Gabriela le dieron.

With the visitors gone, up the stairs Gabriela went.
She had to ready her things for the big event.
Gabriela found her costume under the bed,
but the pretty pink tutu was missing a thread.

Se fueron las visitas y las escaleras Gabriela subió.
Alistarse para su gran evento fue lo que decidió.
Debajo de la cama el traje se encontraba,
pero al lindo tutú rosado un hilo le faltaba.

Gabriela cried, "Oh no! My pretty pink tutu has a big tear!
For my dance recital, now what will I wear?"
Gabriela got needle and thread with tears in her eyes.
But Mami sewed up the costume, to Gabriela's surprise.

Gabriela gritó, «¡Mi lindo tutú rosado se ha empezado a rasgar!
Y ahora, para el recital de danza, ¿qué voy a usar?».
Con lágrimas en los ojos, aguja e hilo Gabriela sacó.
Pero su mamá cosió el traje y Gabriela se sorprendió.

Gabriela tried on her costume to see how it fit,
but the little dancer felt nervous and needed to sit.
Down the hall her grandparents walked. As they approached her room,
they saw Gabriela dressed in her dance costume.

Gabriela se probó el traje para ver cómo le quedaba,
pero se sentó en la cama, pues nerviosa estaba.
En el pasillo caminaban sus abuelos y a su cuarto se acercaron.
Gabriela llevaba su traje de danza cuando ellos la vieron.

Her grandma asked, "Why so glum? Why so down?
Why so sad? Why that frown?"
Gabriela replied, "I'm still nervous. Don't you see?
At my dance recital people might laugh at me."

Su abuela preguntó, «¿Por qué te has deprimido?
¿Por qué estás triste y con el ceño fruncido?».
Gabriela respondió, «Estoy nerviosa. ¿No lo ves?
En el recital de danza, se reirán de mí . . . tal vez».

"But you're a great dancer!" her grandma said,

«Pero, ¡bailas muy bien!», su abuela le hizo notar,

as she helped Gabriela down from the bed.
"Why, thank you, Abuelita! That's nice of you to say.
I'll remember your compliment on my big day."

mientras de la cama a Gabriela la ayudó a bajar.
«Muchísimas gracias, abuelita, por decirme cosas lindas.
Me acordaré de las palabras que me brindas».

Abuelito asked, "When nervous, do you know what I do?
I start by taking a deep breath or two."
Her grandfather added, "Then I close my eyes tight
and envision myself doing everything right."

«¿Sabes qué hago cuando estoy nervioso?
Respiro hondo», dijo su abuelo juicioso,
«y fuerte los ojos tengo que cerrar,
imaginando que hago las cosas sin errar».

Gabriela thanked her grandparents and went
    on her way.
She needed to find her ballet shoes—today!
Gabriela looked and looked and looked
    some more,
before finding her shoes behind the door.

A sus abuelos les agradeció por ayudar.
Y sus zapatillas de ballet se fue a buscar.
Las zapatillas Gabriela buscó y buscó y buscó,
y detrás de la puerta las encontró.

"A pink ribbon for my hair is all I need now."
Gabriela thought, "Almost ready, yet I'm nervous somehow."
Her parents, she realized, would know what to say
to make her feel better in every way.

Gabriela pensó, «Sólo necesito una cinta rosada.
Nerviosa estoy aunque casi preparada».
Seguro sus papás sabrán qué decir
y mucho mejor Gabriela se iba a sentir.

Gabriela asked her parents, "Any advice for me?"
"Hmm," Mami started. "Let me see . . .
Practice makes perfect," she said with a smile.
Papi added, "Your confidence will grow if you practice a while."

Gabriela les preguntó, «¿Algún consejo me quieren compartir?».
Su mamá contestó, «Veamos qué ideas se nos pueden ocurrir».
Sonriendo mami le dijo, «La práctica hace al maestro».
Papi añadió, «Aumentará tu confianza si practicas un rato».

Gabriela went to her bedroom and shut the door.
There she practiced for an hour or more.

A su dormitorio fue y la puerta cerró.
Allí, más de una hora practicando Gabriela se quedó.

She spun and she twirled and she leaped through the air.
She practiced hard, although no one was there.

Hizo piruetas, dio vueltas y por el aire saltó.
Estaba sola esa tarde, pero mucho rato practicó.

Gabriela worked very hard; she gave it her best.
Now less nervous, she decided to rest.
Gabriela went to the kitchen for cold water to drink.
And while gulping it down, she began to think,

Gabriela hizo su mayor esfuerzo mientras practicaba.
Decidió descansar ya que menos nerviosa estaba.
Agua fría a la cocina fue a buscar.
Y mientras la tomaba, Gabriela se puso a pensar,

"All the advice I have followed to the letter."
And about the recital she was feeling much better.
Gabriela was confident and had practiced a lot.
Now her stomach was no longer tied in a knot.

«Todos los consejos he seguido con exactitud».
Sobre el recital, ahora tenía mejor actitud.
Gabriela había practicado mucho y confianza tenía.
Ahora ese nudo en el estómago ya no sentía.

Gabriela imagined herself, once tucked into bed,
dancing well, just like her family had said.
She pictured herself spin, twirl, and leap,
and in no time at all Gabriela was fast asleep.

Una vez acostada, Gabriela pensaba
que, como dijo su familia, bien bailaba.
Saltando y haciendo piruetas se imaginaba,
y al poco tiempo bien dormida Gabriela quedaba.

Gabriela awoke the next morning happy and excited.
It was the day of the recital, and she was delighted!
After eating her breakfast, Gabriela packed up her gear.
She was ready for the show and had nothing to fear.

Al día siguiente, se despertó emocionada.
Era el día del recital y estaba entusiasmada.
Gabriela empacó sus cosas después de desayunar.
¡Ya no tenía miedo y lista se sentía estar!

Later, Gabriela and her family got into the car
to drive to the recital, which wasn't very far.
She thanked her family for their encouragement and praise.
Then it was time for Gabriela to go backstage.

Luego, Gabriela y su familia al carro subieron,
y para ver el recital al teatro todos fueron.
Por haberla animado, a su familia Gabriela agradeció.
Llegó el momento de prepararse y Gabriela se despidió.

Gabriela's family walked into the theater and quickly sat down.
When Gabriela took the stage, there was clapping all around.
In first position Gabriela awaited the music with her head bowed,
until she remembered the advice and peeked up at the crowd.

La familia de Gabriela entró al teatro y rápido se sentó.
Todos aplaudieron cuando al escenario Gabriela salió.
Esperando la música en primera posición, la cabeza Gabriela inclinó.
Se acordó de los consejos y un vistazo al público Gabriela le dio.

When the music started, Gabriela had a confident smile on her face.

La música comenzó y Gabriela sonrió con confianza.

She performed pirouettes and arabesques with beauty and grace.

Hizo piruetas y arabescos con mucha elegancia.

Gabriela danced perfectly! Not one mistake did she make.
Applause filled the air, and bow after bow Gabriela had to take.

¡Gabriela danzó maravillosamente! Ni una vez se equivocó.
Tanto aplaudieron que varias veces ante el público Gabriela saludó.

Personalized Children's Books from Snowflake Stories™

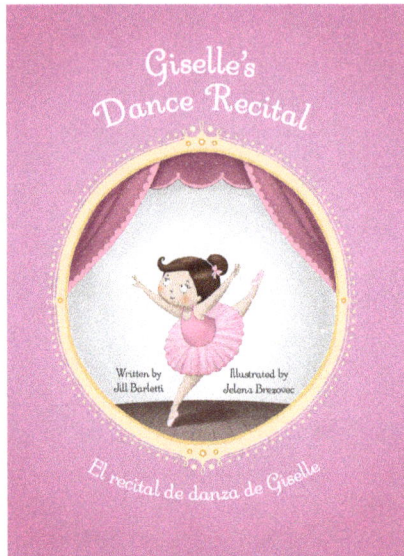

International Latino Book Award (2)
National Indie Excellence Award
Moonbeam Children's Book Award

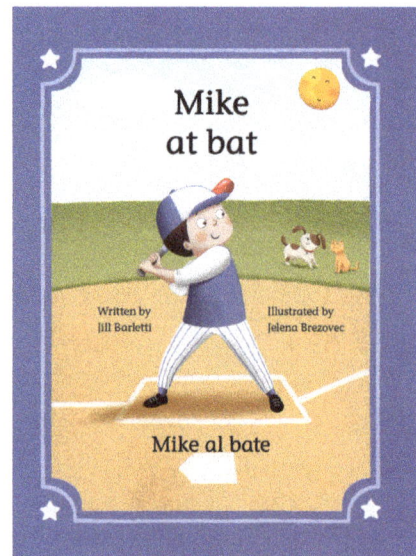

International Latino Book Award (5)
National Indie Excellence Award

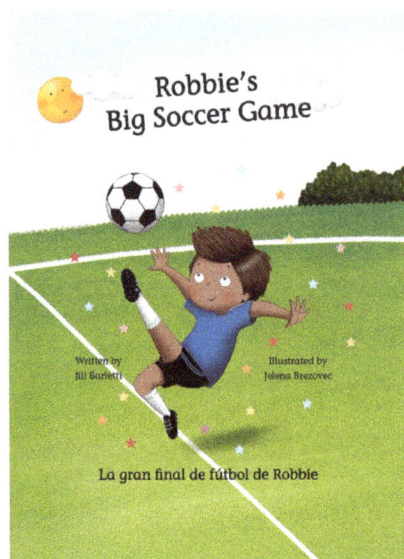

International Latino Book Award (5)
National Indie Excellence Award
Foreword Review's Foreword INDIES